THE WAY TO PRAY

STEPHEN CHAPPELL

A previous edition of this book was published in 2011 by Coastline Baptist
Church under the title *When You Pray*. This updated and edited edition
was first published in 2022 by Striving Together Publications, a ministry
of Lancaster Baptist Church, Lancaster, CA 93535. Striving Together
Publications is committed to providing tried, trusted, and proven books that
will further equip local churches to carry out the Great Commission. Your
comments and suggestions are valued.

Striving Together Publications
4020 E. Lancaster Blvd.
Lancaster, CA 93535
800.201.7748

Cover design by Stephen Houk
Writing assistance by Lesley Gonzalez

The contents of this book are the result of decades of
spiritual growth in life and ministry. It is not our intent
to claim originality with any quote or thought that could not
readily be tied to an original source.

ISBN 978-1-59894-473-0 (paperback)
ISBN 978-1-59894-474-7 (ebook)

Printed in the United States of America

The Lord's Prayer

After this manner therefore pray ye:
Our Father which art in heaven,
Hallowed be thy name.

Thy kingdom come.
Thy will be done in earth, as it is in heaven.

Give us this day our daily bread.

And forgive us our debts,
as we forgive our debtors.

And lead us not into temptation,
but deliver us from evil:
For thine is the kingdom, and the power,
and the glory, for ever. Amen.

—Matthew 6:9–13

Contents

After this manner therefore pray ye:
Our Father which art in heaven,
Hallowed be thy name.
—Matthew 6:9

ONE

Pray Ye

Do you remember how you spent your time in 2020? If you're like many Americans, you devoted more time to reading and learning than ever before. According to the US Department of Labor, the amount of time Americans older than fifteen spent reading increased 21 percent in the last half of that year.[1] Not coincidentally, this was the same period many Americans were still at home waiting out the COVID-19 pandemic. Book sale records suggest they read to gain new skills for schooling their children, broaden their job prospects, improve their relationships, and manage stress, among other reasons.[2]

While I have not always enjoyed reading for its own sake, it is a habit I have developed when I have specific areas of need in my life. Whenever I need advice or additional perspectives on anything from marriage and family relationships to leadership and more, I often turn to books to help me evaluate and sometimes change how I approach these areas in my life.

Anyone who, like me, has spent considerable time browsing the reference shelves of a bookstore or searching resources online knows there are a great number of books available to call our attention to the topic of prayer. Ironically, when I see them I've often thought, "I'd love to learn more about prayer—but I just have too much going on right now. Maybe when I get my other needs all squared away, I'll have some time." In reality, this logic exposes a common misconception: that when we finally have our lives where they should be—when we have at last managed our stress, improved our relationships, paid our bills, and summoned the strength to quit our bad habits—then we will be in the perfect position to get closer to God through prayer.

But God, in His love for us, teaches us to look at this differently. In effect, He says, "Don't waste time trying to handle things that I have not equipped you to handle. Come to Me, and we'll take care of it together." You see, prayer is the God-designed avenue through which we gain the insight and resources we need to live the lives He has given us.

You may already be familiar with one of the most well-known prayers in the Bible. This prayer, found in the Gospel of Matthew and paralleled in the Gospel of Luke, is sometimes called "the Lord's Prayer." Jesus taught it to His disciples, who had by this time observed Christ do amazing works. They had seen His miracles. They had heard Him preach and teach, captivating crowds of thousands. They watched Him quiet storms, walk on water, and care for people on a personal level. And somewhere along the way, these men who formed the core of Jesus' ministry team had also watched Him pray.

Of course, they already knew about prayer. They would have established a habit of praying every day in keeping with the Old Testament laws. But there was something different about the prayers of Christ, something different about the way He talked with God the Father. And there was something different about the way His prayers were answered. It's hardly a wonder, then, that they asked Him to show them how to pray as He did.

Some people believe prayer to be a little like asking wishes of a genie, the magical creature of folklore and fairy tales that is released when someone stumbles upon a tell-tale lamp and gives it a rub. We understand almost without being told that no matter how many wishes the genie grants, there is inevitably a limit. The lucky finder can't just form unlimited wishes; it doesn't work that way. The code must be followed.

Prayer doesn't work that way, either. God is no genie waiting to perform miraculous works for our amusement. But through prayer, we do find an open invitation to confidently make our way into His presence to find help in our time of need. And unlike a genie, there are no restrictions on the number of things we can ask of God. As we'll see, though, prayer is not about getting our will accomplished through the power of Heaven or in our lives on earth. It is about a relationship with Him.

The disciples discerned that everything that happened in Christ's ministry was made possible through prayer. They realized that if they learned how to pray they would gain the tools to do the work they were called to do. In Luke 11 we find that it was the disciples who approached Jesus, asking to learn how to pray.

> And it came to pass, that, as he was praying in a certain place, when he ceased, one of his disciples said unto him, Lord, teach us to pray, as John also taught his disciples.—Luke 11:1

They were saying, "We've never seen anything like this before. We need to learn how to have this type of connection with God the Father in our lives." So Jesus took the time to teach these men how to talk with God. His instructions are just as applicable today to us who yearn to connect with God and be equipped for the lives to which He has called us.

Follow the Pattern

Communication is never an easy thing. Sometimes it can get downright tricky. I once saw a sign outside a restroom that read, *"Toilet broken—use floor below."* Thankfully, I was able to understand the intent of the message and make the right decision. But this is a great illustration of the fact that even our best attempts at communication sometimes only complicate the message.

When it comes to communicating with God, we don't have to worry about mixed messages because we have been given a pattern to follow:

> After this manner therefore pray ye:—Matthew 6:9

In this verse Jesus indicates that His short, simply-worded prayer is a pattern for us—not necessarily to repeat from rote memory, but to use and learn from as a guide. When it comes to prayer, I can make a mess of things, but the picture painted by Christ in this model prayer is that of a child going to his father. When we begin to understand that prayer is a privilege God has given to His children, we can find comfort and confidence in His call to "Pray ye."

In the following pages, we're going to explore Jesus' instructions for prayer line by line. But first, we need to look specifically at our relationship with Him. After all, His invitation to pray is based on God being our Father.

Communication Block

Have you ever wondered where you *really* stand with God? The basis for healthy communication with God is an absolute confidence in our relationship with Him as Father.

I'll never forget the Sunday I attended church years ago and heard a guest speaker from Arkansas who asked a question that really bothered me: "Do you know for sure that if you died today, you'd go to Heaven?" The fact was, I really didn't know. I couldn't honestly be sure that God was my heavenly Father.

You see, I have a problem—and you do, too. This problem creates a chasm between us and God. This not only affects our prayers, but it affects our very relationship with God. What is this problem we all have in common? It's simple: we are all sinners.

> As it is written, There is none righteous, no, not one:
> —Romans 3:10

> For all have sinned, and come short of the glory of God;—Romans 3:23

No one had to teach us how to sin; we received no training to be able to lie, think wrong thoughts, or even be selfish. We were just born that way. This is evident in the story of the brother and sister who were playing on a kiddie horse ride outside a grocery store. The boy, irritated that he had to share the ride with his sister, said, "You know, if one of us would get off, there would be more room for me."

The question of why we are so prone to sin can be understood if we consider a similar question: How does a worm get inside an apple? You might think the worm burrows in from the outside, but scientists have discovered that this is not the case. In truth, the worm grew inside the apple. And how did it get in there? Simple! An insect lays an egg in the apple blossom, and sometime later the worm hatches in the heart of the apple and then eats its way out. Like the worm, sin begins in the heart and works its way out through our thoughts, words, and actions. I wish I had known this when I was growing up. Whenever I did something wrong and my mom asked, "Son, what has gotten into you?" I could have said, "Nothing! It's just the worms working their way out!"

Each of us arrives on this planet with a desire to go and have our own way. Years ago when my daughters were still at home, I happened to overhear an argument between them. I listened to them trading zingers for awhile because it was entertaining, but I thought, "Where is this coming from? They must get it from their mother." Of course this wasn't the case; I'm sure I contributed plenty! But ultimately, we inherit our sinful nature from our common father, the first man, Adam. The Bible tells us,

> Wherefore, as by one man sin entered into the world, and death by sin; and so death passed upon all men, for that all have sinned.—Romans 5:12

It's not really news to any of us that we are sinners. We all know that we aren't perfect and don't measure up to God's standards. But the Bible is clear that there is a penalty for being a sinner:

> For the wages of sin is death; but the gift of God
> is eternal life through Jesus Christ our Lord.
> —Romans 6:23

God is perfect and holy. We are imperfect sinners. This is where the breach of communication comes. We know there is a separation between us and God, and we are not always sure how to know that the connection is there. How can we know that He is listening when we pray? More specifically, how can we know that we are His children and He is our heavenly Father?

Become Part of the Family of God

This issue of making sure that we are connected to God through a relationship that will last forever is dealt with in great depth in the Bible. In fact, in the Gospel of John we meet a man who came to Jesus to talk about this. Christ's response to him gives us one of the most well-known and loved verses in Scripture.

When we first read of Nicodemus in John 3, we find that he was quite a guy. The Bible describes him as a "Pharisee," "a ruler of the Jews," and "a master of Israel." These words tell us that Nicodemus was super religious and very knowledgeable in the Scriptures. He was a highly-educated teacher and a powerful, politically-connected figure. In many ways Nicodemus was the very best Jewish society had to offer. But even so, he could not be sure that God was his heavenly Father.

Nicodemus came to Jesus at night, and it would not be farfetched to suppose he did so to avoid being seen. Jesus told him,

> ... Verily, verily, I say unto thee, Except a man be born again, he cannot see the kingdom of God.—John 3:3

Of course, this makes great sense to us; to have God as your Father, you must be born into His family. But Nicodemus had never heard the expression "born again" before.

> ... How can a man be born when he is old? can he enter the second time into his mother's womb, and be born?—John 3:4

He totally missed the point, but that happens sometimes. Christians use many expressions to refer to a relationship with God—*born again, saved,* or *ask Jesus into your heart*—that are unfamiliar to unbelievers. I heard of a little girl who was learning about this in Sunday School. That afternoon as she lay with her cheek to her mother's heart she asked, "Mom, do you have Jesus in your heart?"

"Yes, I do," replied the girl's mother.

The girl listened quietly for a moment and said, "It sounds like He's making coffee."

This little girl was just trying to understand, just like Nicodemus. To help Nicodemus, Jesus said:

> ...Verily, verily, I say unto thee, Except a man be born of water and of the Spirit, he cannot enter into the kingdom of God. That which is born of the flesh is flesh; and that which is born of the Spirit is spirit. Marvel not that I said unto thee, Ye must be born again.—John 3:5–7

By now Jesus has told Nicodemus three times that one "must be born again." Now, He further explains that we are all born physically and we are all the children of an earthly father. But we must be born spiritually if we are to enjoy a relationship with our heavenly Father—a God who accepts, forgives, helps, assures us of a home in Heaven as well as a life of purpose on Earth, and hears and answers our prayers.

Nowhere do we find in the Bible that being "born again" or establishing a relationship with God is a result of our good works like joining a church, giving an offering, getting baptized, or anything else. In fact, we learn that a relationship with God is only found one way:

> Not by works of righteousness which we have done, but according to his mercy he saved us, by the washing of regeneration, and renewing of the Holy Ghost; —Titus 3:5

Jesus told Nicodemus exactly how this is possible:

> That whosoever believeth in him should not perish, but have eternal life. For God so loved the world, that he gave his only begotten Son, that whosoever believeth in him should not perish, but have everlasting life. —John 3:15–16

When we are born again, we receive a new life that is eternal and can never be taken away—all based on belief, or faith. How do we get it? We find clear direction on this in many Bible passages, but one of my favorites is in Romans.

> That if thou shalt confess with thy mouth the Lord Jesus, and shalt believe in thine heart that God hath raised him from the dead, thou shalt be saved. For with the heart man believeth unto righteousness; and with the mouth confession is made unto salvation. For the scripture saith, Whosoever believeth on him shall not be ashamed. For there is no difference between the Jew and the Greek: for the same Lord over all is rich unto all that call upon him. For whosoever shall call upon the name of the Lord shall be saved.—Romans 10:9–13

We all come to God the same way: by faith, which we express by "calling" on Him for salvation. We admit that we are sinners, acknowledge that Jesus paid for our sins through His death and resurrection, and accept His free gift of eternal life. Then are we "born again" and God becomes our Father.

I once heard a story that broke my heart. A soldier who was finally coming home from war called his parents to ask a favor: "I have a friend I'd like to bring with me."

"Sure," they replied. "We'd love to meet him."

"There's something you should know," the son continued. "My friend was hurt pretty badly in the fighting. He stepped on a land mine and lost an arm and a leg. He has nowhere else to go, and I want him to come live with us."

"We're sorry to hear that, son. Maybe we can help him find somewhere to live."

"No, I want him to live with us," the son insisted.

"You don't know what you're asking," his father replied. "Someone with such problems would be a terrible burden on us. We have our own lives to live, and you should let him live his. Just come home. He'll figure something out."

The son hung up the phone and did not contact his parents again. Weeks turned into months and then into more than a year. One day, the soldier's parents received a call from the police notifying them of their son's death and asking them to come identify the body. At the city morgue, the grief-stricken parents were shown the body of a man they recognized as their son. To their horror, they discovered the body was missing one arm and one leg.

The parents in this story are like many of us. We find it easy to love those who are loveable and all put together, or who have something to offer us. Yet, how many of us are always loveable? How many of us have ourselves together and can offer others anything of value? God doesn't love that way. He has no interest in seeing us go through life as spiritual orphans. He wants to be here for us. He knows our hurts, trials, and failures, and He still invites us to come to Him.

I was born at a Kaiser hospital in Santa Clara, California. I have the birth record to prove it. That record lists my father's name as Larry. But I have another birth record—of the day that I placed my faith in Christ for salvation and was born again into His family. The record for this birth is kept in Heaven, and it lists God as my Father. Before that day, I knew what religion was all about, but I didn't really know what a relationship with God was about.

A relationship with God, and by extension a healthy prayer life, begins when we accept His love and forgiveness and are born again. Have you settled that matter? Have you been assured of that family connection that makes God your Father?

If you have not, I encourage you to make the choice today to place your faith in Christ. Becoming a child of God is as simple as confessing to Him that you are a sinner in need of His payment on the cross for your sin and calling out to Him for salvation. He invites,

> For whosoever shall call upon the name of the Lord shall be saved.—Romans 10:13

That is a promise directly from God that if you will pray to Him, confess that you are a sinner, ask Him to forgive your sins, and turn to Him alone to be your Savior; He promises to save you and make you His son or daughter. You can make that decision today by praying from your heart, something like this:

> Dear God, I know that I am separated from you because of sin. I confess that in my sin, I cannot save myself. Right now, I turn to you alone to be my Savior. I ask you to save me from the penalty of my sin, and I trust you to provide eternal life to me. Amen.

The Way to Pray

Whether you have just become God's child or you already knew God as your Father, I pray that this book will be a help to you in growing in your relationship with Him through the amazing resource of prayer.

Father, thank You for Your love and grace. Thank You for sending Your only Son, Jesus, so that through faith in Him I can have an eternal relationship with You. I pray that my life as Your child would be pleasing to You.

After this manner therefore pray ye:
Our Father which art in heaven,
Hallowed be thy name.
—Matthew 6:9

TWO

Our Father

We may have known it before, but we have all seen through our collective pandemic experiences how incredibly important it is that we have meaningful connections to other people; in fact, we can't live—at least, not well—without them.[1] One relationship I wouldn't be the same without is the one I have with my wife. She just "gets" me. Sometimes I don't even need to tell her how I'm feeling; she understands without me having to say a word. Sometimes I just know how she is feeling as well, but she always tells me anyhow. (She likes to talk more than I do.) Because we have a special connection, I "get" her, too.

The next verses in our passage deal with our connection to God. The interesting thing about having a close relationship with God is that He shows us through that connection how to make the most of all our other relationships. He already knows all there is to know about marriage because He invented it. He knows about the family because it was His idea. The challenges of friendship and professional relationships? He's been there and done that. Jesus had all these experiences and can thus serve as a guide for us:

> For we have not an high priest which cannot be touched with the feeling of our infirmities; but was in all points tempted like as we are, yet without sin.
> —Hebrews 4:15

We can't tell Jesus that He doesn't understand what we are going through because He does. He knows joy, disappointment, friendship, and rejection. He truly longs to go through our lives with us, providing the insight that we need each step of the way.

In relationships of any kind, there is nothing more important than communication. So it only makes sense that a close relationship with God requires an understanding of prayer. When we pray, we're communicating with the Creator of the universe. Jesus' example given in the Lord's Prayer teaches us how to talk with God and how to hear from God.

When the topic of prayer comes up, we often ask the same questions. How should a prayer begin? How should it end? Should we stand, sit, or kneel? Should we bow our heads and fold our hands as we teach small children to do? Do our eyes really have to be closed, or can God hear us when they're open? There's nothing wrong with these questions, but they can reveal misconceptions about our connection with God. We can easily become so involved in analyzing the form of prayer that we miss its function, more concerned about looking and sounding "right" than praying from the heart.

The disciples surely had some of the same questions. For this reason, Jesus took the time to give us answers.

The Real Rules of Prayer

As we saw in Chapter 1, Jesus' followers already knew some things about prayer. What they knew, however, was not altogether correct. Jesus needed to address the misconceptions they had learned along the way with a few guidelines.

Prayer must be regular. Jesus repeatedly says the phrase "and when you pray" in the first nine verses of Matthew 6. Clearly, He was making a point that prayer will never work if we don't do it. While this may sound simple enough, prayer is the single most difficult spiritual discipline and the one that gets the least attention. But consider this: the prayers we never get around to praying have no power in our lives. That is why Jesus said,

> ...Ask, and it shall be given you; seek, and ye shall find; knock, and it shall be opened unto you.
> —Luke 11:9

It's also why James, the half-brother of Jesus, wrote,

> ...ye have not, because ye ask not.—James 4:2

It is not enough to know *about* prayer; we will never discover the blessings in it that God intended for us if we don't *pray*. Prayer must be a regular part of our lives. In fact, the Apostle Paul said God's people should pray "without ceasing" (1 Thessalonians 5:17).

Prayer must be real. Jesus warned against prayers such as those made by the religious leaders of the day, intended more for public audiences than for God:

> Take heed that ye do not your alms before men, to be seen of them: otherwise ye have no reward of your Father which is in heaven...And when thou prayest, thou shalt not be as the hypocrites are: for they love to pray standing in the synagogues and in the corners of

the streets, that they may be seen of men. Verily I say
unto you, They have their reward.—Matthew 6:1, 5

These prayers are a charade, and God has no use for
them. He's not impressed with our oratory skills. He wants
to hear the expressions of our hearts—sincere, honest,
and real.

Prayer must be relational. In Matthew 6:9 Jesus told
the disciples to pray to God as "our Father," a familial link
that would have been news to them. They knew God was
their Father in theory, but they had not experienced such a
relationship in reality. Their prayers would have consisted
of a memorized passage from the Old Testament called the
Shema, which employs some of the many Old Testament
names for God. They would have prayed to Elohim, which
means "powerful God," to Adonai, which means "Lord,"
and to El Shaddai or Jehovah Jireh, which mean "the
Almighty" and "God our Provider." But...praying to "our
Father"?

Use of the name "Father" shows us that our connection
to God is not about religion, science, or a formula. It is
about a relationship. Jesus' prayer to His Father mere hours
before He would be unfairly tried and ultimately crucified
shows this:

> ...Abba, Father, all things are possible unto thee; take away this cup from me: nevertheless not what I will, but what thou wilt.—Mark 14:36

The word *Abba* is an Aramaic term that can be translated as "Daddy" or "Papa." Jesus used it as a child's way of crying out to a dad who could do anything. If we have established a connection to God through salvation, we have the same relationship.

> For ye have not received the spirit of bondage again to fear; but ye have received the Spirit of adoption, whereby we cry, Abba, Father.—Romans 8:15

Finding Comfort in Prayer

From everything we know about God, we can correctly assume He would not call us to do anything "just because" or tell us to do something "without ceasing" if it had no practical value for us. And Paul gives us one of the reasons prayer should take priority in our lives:

> Blessed be God, even the Father of our Lord Jesus Christ, the Father of mercies, and the God of all comfort;—2 Corinthians 1:3

Everything about the process of prayer brings us comfort simply because of to whom our prayers are directed. When we pray to God we are praying to the source of comfort.

Comfort in our community. I love the plural possessiveness of the phrase "*our* Father." In fact, the Lord's Prayer is full of plural pronouns:

- Give *us* this day *our* daily bread
- Forgive *us our* debts as *we* forgive *our* debtors
- Lead *us* not into temptation
- Deliver *us* from evil

Among other things, prayer is a reminder that we are part of a family. We are not in this life alone; not only do we have a God who will "never leave or forsake" us (Joshua 1:5; Hebrews 13:5), but we also have a community of brothers and sisters who can support us and pray for and with us. As independent as we may feel at times, we all need a family—and the family of faith is one that can bring us joy as we go through life together.

I know all too well what it's like to find comfort in the family of faith and to be encouraged beyond words by someone sharing that they were praying for me. One of my best friends is a pastor. I once felt led of the Lord to send him a note along with a book I thought might be useful to him at some point. This excerpt is from an email he sent a few days later:

> I had "one of those lunches" yesterday, where I was taken to task by a young gentleman, and made aware of some comments that had been going around... gossip, really. My relationships were called into question, and my wife was hit pretty hard as well. Needless to say, I had to handle it to some degree and have had overwhelmingly positive feedback concerning shutting down the garbage. Anyway, I had the wind totally taken out of my sails, dealt with a real gut punch, was dealing with having to straighten out some lies... walked in my door just prior to a church service to a book from you... and a note claiming I had a friend and that you were praying. God is awesome! It did more than you know.

When I sent that package, I had no idea what my friend was going through. That's just how God works—He uses us, the community of faith, to help each other in times of need.

Comfort in our confidence. Another word that gives us comfort seems at first glance relatively insignificant. Matthew 6:9 says, "Our Father which *art* in Heaven." What a reminder that God *is*.

Years before Jesus spent time teaching the disciples about prayer, God appeared in a burning bush to a man named Moses. When Moses asked God for His name, God answered:

> And God said unto Moses, I AM THAT I AM: and he said, Thus shalt thou say unto the children of Israel, I AM hath sent me unto you.—Exodus 3:14

God was saying that He is the eternally-existent, completely self-sufficient, all-powerful God who is anything and everything that we could ever need in life. We can have confidence when we go to God in prayer because He *is* and because of *who* He is: our Father.

When I was growing up, I always knew I could go to my dad for help whenever I got myself in a jam. He helped every time—not always in the way I would have imagined, but always in the way that was best for me. How much more so is my heavenly Father here for me! How much more so is He there for you!

Comfort in God's control. The first words of the Lord's Prayer tell us "Our Father" is "in Heaven," but God is literally everywhere at the same time. The psalmist writes,

> Thou compassest my path and my lying down, And art acquainted with all my ways.—Psalm 139:3

The mention of Heaven in Matthew 6:9 speaks not of God's location but of His authority and the reality that He is above all of our problems. You see, although our lives can seem to be out of control, they are under His care. Whatever you are going through, even on the worst day of your life, I can tell you that God is up to the challenge. One of the great benefits of life's trials is that they often direct us to God and we learn that we can trust Him completely. This thought should bring comfort and immeasurable joy.

A. C. Dixon once wrote, "When we rely upon organization, we get what organization can do; when we rely upon education, we get what education can do; when we rely upon eloquence, we get what eloquence can do, and so on. I am not disposed to undervalue any of these things in their proper place, but when we rely upon prayer, we get what God can do."[2]

Making a Connection

We've spent considerable time on the "how" of a relationship with God. Now, let's take a moment to think about the "what." It is imperative that we are certain we have a connection with God through faith in Christ, but what does that connection mean for our prayers?

Prayer has power. I remember a time when I was in a valley of decision. I was sitting at my desk when I received a call from a nationally-known pastor. For me, a call from this man was a big deal. I shared my heart and listened intently to his counsel, feeling I was talking to someone who was "in the know." I was somewhat in awe that this man would communicate with me. Afterward, I thought about telling God about the call—and then it dawned on me that communicating with God is of so much higher value that every other conversation pales in comparison.

I don't say this to denigrate wise counsel that can come from our fellow believers, which we certainly need. Neither do I mean any disrespect to this pastor, who is now in Heaven. It was kind of him to call, and it meant so much that he took the time to talk to me. But when we are talking to God, we are talking to the source of *all power in the entire universe.* Shouldn't that mean so much more?

Prayer has potential. Among my greatest desires is that my children do well in life. I will do everything within my power to help them, although I'm often reminded that my power and resources have limits. But when God is our Father, there are no limits. He can help us in every area of life. We will never have a need that is beyond His power or outside His expertise. He is God, and He loves His children. The Apostle John wrote,

> Beloved, now are we the sons of God, and it doth not yet appear what we shall be: but we know that, when he shall appear, we shall be like him; for we shall see him as he is.—1 John 3:2

God accepts us as we are, but He is ever working within us so that His will can be worked through us.

> Ye are of God, little children, and have overcome them: because greater is he that is in you, than he that is in the world.—1 John 4:4

Sometimes, prayer can be hindered. Remember those cell phone commercials where someone was always asking "Can you hear me now?" Cell phone technology is pretty impressive these days, but even the best phone can miss a connection due to poor network coverage, geography, or bad weather. Our connection with God isn't impacted by how many tall trees are around us, but like all relationships, it can suffer if we don't invest in it.

My granddad told me years ago to always buy John Deere tractors and Ford trucks. I haven't yet had the need for a tractor, but I have had several Fords over the years. As good as Ford trucks are (they're the best!), they are not perfect. I was once driving my truck and noticed a lack of power. I just couldn't peel out as easily as I once could. In time, the power dropped off even more, so I took the truck in for a checkup. I discovered there was a problem with my catalytic converter, which decreases engine emissions that are harmful to the environment. As my catalytic converter broke it became clogged, and trying to push exhaust out of a clogged pipe affected the power of the entire engine.

Sin can clog the connection between us and our Father that gives power to our lives. Our sin does not make God any less our Father or us any less His children, but it does make our communication strained and disconnected. And while our connection with God cannot be severed once we become His children, our sins can breach the fellowship. But we have a way to restore the connection:

> If we confess our sins, he is faithful and just to forgive us our sins, and to cleanse us from all unrighteousness.—1 John 1:9

Unlike cell phones or vehicles, prayer always works. Jesus told His disciples,

> . . . Verily, verily, I say unto you, Whatsoever ye shall ask the Father in my name, he will give it you. —John 16:23

The Way to Pray

If you are feeling a loss of power or connection to God through prayer, perhaps you should examine your life to see if your connection could be improved by confessing and forsaking sin. When we let our Father know that we have sinned, He will restore that closeness again.

Or perhaps you cannot restore a close connection with God because you have not yet established a relationship with Him through faith. There is no time like the present. Turn to Him now—He's always listening for your call.

Father, thank You for the privilege of prayer. How grateful I am for Jesus who teaches us how we ought to pray. The thought that I'm praying to my heavenly Father who is seated upon the throne of the universe while at the same time working in my life brings me joy, hope, and peace.

Thy kingdom come.
Thy will be done in earth,
as it is in heaven.
—Matthew 6:9

THREE

Thy Will Be Done

Years ago, I had the privilege of working for a man who taught me a great deal. He gave clear directions, provided the necessary resources to succeed, and believed employees should have the liberty to take ownership of their work and "sink or swim" on their own merits. He also had an open door policy, of which I took advantage. But one day I remember walking in a little too cavalierly, with an attitude that suggested I was perhaps taking our working relationship too lightly. My boss had no problem reminding me that he was the one in charge. I was allowed into his office because of his grace. I had been hired to accomplish his goals. His availability was a great benefit to me, but at the end of the day I did well to remember that he was calling the shots, for which he deserved a measure of respect.

A healthy prayer life is built on a relationship with God, "our Father," through faith, and this is a relationship we are not to take lightly, either. We are blessed by it to confidently enter into His presence, and we are invited to cry out to Him as children would to an earthly father, but we must never forget we are speaking to Almighty God! The words "Thy kingdom" and "Thy will" in Matthew 6:10 should remind us that He is in control and the purpose of our very existence is to please Him.

There seems to be a general consensus in our society that humankind is basically good and that if we work hard enough, together we can solve our problems. That understanding makes for good speeches and warm, fuzzy feelings, but it is very different from what we read in the Bible, which is that all people are totally depraved and born with a sin nature. The Bible teaches that try as we might, apart from God, we simply don't have what it takes to solve the problems that plague humanity.

Our society also tries to perpetuate the myth that together we can create some sort of a social nirvana where justice reigns supreme in a world teeming with peace. Of course, I'm a proponent of justice and peace. But if we take an honest look at our world we see an utter lack of justice and total absence of peace, and the picture is not improving despite the efforts of some of our "best" philosophers and activists. The Bible tells us what the world will look like prior to the return of Christ:

> And Jesus answered and said unto them, Take heed that no man deceive you. For many shall come in my name, saying, I am Christ; and shall deceive many. And ye shall hear of wars and rumours of wars: see that ye be not troubled: for all these things must come to pass, but the end is not yet. For nation shall rise against nation, and kingdom against kingdom: and there shall be famines, and pestilences, and earthquakes, in divers places. All these are the beginning of sorrows.
> —Matthew 24:4–8

As humankind tries to create its ideal world, there is an inevitable attempt to fashion "man" as a controlling and determining figure we think resembles God. The problem is that the inevitable byproduct of deifying man is humanizing God. Rather than giving God the respect He deserves, He becomes "the man upstairs" or worse—a distant, unknowable being who is disinterested in the affairs of man.

Conversely, sincere prayer acknowledges that we desperately need God. In prayer we can venture into His presence, admitting our need of His wisdom and power in our lives. When done correctly, there is nothing more humbling or faith-filled than bending a knee in reverential prayer.

Honor His Name

...Our Father which art in heaven, Hallowed be thy name.—Matthew 6:9

The term *hallowed* in the verse above means "dedicated, honorable, or holy".[1] God's name is such a great name and so worthy of honor that He dedicated one of His original ten commandments to set it apart and has always been protective of it:

Thou shalt not take the name of the LORD thy God in vain; for the LORD will not hold him guiltless that taketh his name in vain.—Exodus 20:7

And I will sanctify my great name, which was profaned among the heathen, which ye have profaned in the midst of them; and the heathen shall know that I am the LORD, saith the Lord GOD, when I shall be sanctified in you before their eyes.—Ezekiel 36:23

When we go to God and recognize that His very name is holy, we are making a decision. Our decision doesn't make Him holy; that was settled in eternity past. Our decision communicates our love and respect for Him.

If we carry the name of God with us as we go through life, it changes us. My father used to caution me when I was growing up about taking our family name seriously. A name carries with it the weight of reputation, and I was to do my part to keep our name out of places and situations it should not go, to ensure it continued to represent something of which our family could be proud.

If our earthly family names are so important, how much more so is the name of our heavenly Father? We should be ever careful to take His name seriously. Our careless or casual vain use of God's name through cursing or expressions of surprise indicates not only that we don't value His name, but also that we don't have the respectful, reverential view of God that we should.

> But I say unto you, That every idle word that men shall speak, they shall give account thereof in the day of judgment.—Matthew 12:36

It should bother every true believer when we hear the name of our God spoken with anything less than the love and respect He deserves. Honoring God's name in prayers and in our conversations reveals hearts that long to honor His name in our lives.

Focus on His Kingdom

Thy kingdom come… —Matthew 6:10

The next words in this model prayer are some of my favorites. Think of what our prayer has essentially been to this point: "God, You are our Father. You are in the seat of power and authority in Heaven, and we honor You for who You are." Now we continue to say, "We are so excited for the day when You will come to rule on Earth."

The kingdom spoken of in this verse is a millennial one in which Christ will rule and reign—and be assured that it is coming.

And as ye go, preach, saying, The kingdom of heaven is at hand.—Matthew 10:7

He which testifieth these things saith, Surely I come quickly. Amen. Even so, come, Lord Jesus. —Revelation 22:20

Our prayer, then, is "God, we believe in You, and we know that the day is coming when this earthly system will be abolished and You will rule and reign over us. Oh, how we long for it to happen soon!"

I love the fact that while the promises of God encourage our prayers, the prayers we offer that are based upon His promises encourage the heart of God. Longing and living for the kingdom of God will radically change our lives. You see, if our focus is on His kingdom, we won't be worried about trying to build one of our own.

> But seek ye first the kingdom of God, and his righteousness; and all these things shall be added unto you.—Matthew 6:33

There's a story about a farmer who told his wife that he was going out to his fields to harvest all the fruit that had ripened. He woke up early the next morning so he could warm up his truck—then he noticed that he was nearly out of gas. He decided to take a detour to the gas station to fill up. Once he'd returned, he remembered the pigs hadn't been fed, so he took another detour to the corn crib to grab some feed sacks. Beside the feed sacks he found potatoes that had sprouted and decided to take another detour to the potato pit. He was headed to the potato pit when he passed his woodpile and remembered that his wife had been asking for more firewood. So he spent some time splitting extra logs and piled them into the wheelbarrow.

On his way to deliver the wood, he saw the door to the chicken coop was hanging off its hinges. By the time he'd finished repairing the door, inspecting the potatoes, and feeding the pigs, the day was half gone and he hadn't even gotten out to his fruit fields. He had become so focused on the little tasks that he missed the main objective.

How often do we do the same thing? We can easily get so "dialed in" on our own lives and issues that we miss the main objective. God's kingdom will come, and we are to desire its coming and live with that fact in mind. A healthy prayer life is based on this understanding.

Seek His Will

> . . . Thy will be done in earth, as it is in heaven.
> —Matthew 6:10

What does it mean to pray that God's will be done? Christ not only modeled this for us here, but He prayed this way as well. One example is His prayer in the Garden of Gethsemane:

> Saying, Father, if thou be willing, remove this cup from me: nevertheless not my will, but thine, be done.
> —Luke 22:42

According to Christ's example, praying that God's "will be done in earth as it is in heaven," is expressing a desire that His purpose be accomplished, beginning in our hearts. We are saying, "Lord, let us carry out Your will in our lives so we may touch the world." If we have decided that He is the holy God, and if we have a desire for Him to reign, then we find a duty to do what pleases Him and furthers His will.

When we pray for God's will to be done we are saying, "God, take our lives and let our influence for You make Earth a little more like Heaven." Have you ever wondered how God's will is carried out in Heaven, as the text says? The behavior of the angels gives us some great insight into this. In the Christmas narrative, the angel tells Zacharias,

> …I am Gabriel, that stand in the presence of God; and am sent to speak unto thee, and to shew thee these glad tidings.—Luke 1:19

If we are sincerely interested in honoring the name of God, seeing His kingdom come, and doing His will, then like the angels, we'll have to yield our lives to Him. He is our heavenly Father, but at the same time He is the King, which means we are His subjects.

We will all go through many times of trial and disappointment in life. I remember a particular incident when I was younger and greatly disappointed by something that had gone spectacularly wrong. I had it all figured out, but nothing had gone according to plan. I'd placed confidence in people who let me down, but worse, I'd let myself down. As you can imagine, I was upset. I spent some time stewing over what I felt was my bad fortune. I don't know that I became bitter, but I was definitely in danger of bitterness soon down the road. I was spinning my wheels, wasting time, and becoming increasingly selfish.

But God had been working on my heart during this time, and He helped me see that I had lost sight of the truth that He is God. It was such a simple realization, but I was amazed by the conviction I felt as I began to evaluate my actions against the backdrop of His holiness. Then and there I decided that He would be in charge of my path once again, and a wonderful thing happened. I began to want His kingdom to come, and I wanted it to come first to my heart.

My prayer life changed when my heart changed. I found myself saying, "Father, You are holy. Your kingdom is greater than anything I could do in life. Your will is my calling. Take this broken plan and put it together in the way that pleases You most." To be honest, I thought that prayer would lead me into more heartache and that I would never have or accomplish anything of value, but would instead have to settle for something else. I have to tell you that the opposite was my experience. I found a fulfillment and joy return to my life. God's way is always best.

True victory in life comes from praying the words of this passage from our hearts. As we pray to be used to further God's kingdom and according to His will, we'll find that our loving Father is ready, willing, and able to take our lives and use them in ways that will amaze us for His glory. He is a great God. Do you know Him? Is He ruling in your life? Why don't you give Him reign to do so beginning today?

Father, help me to live in such a way that I reflect
Your holy name in a good way. It is a joy beyond belief to
know that Your kingdom is coming, and I'm looking forward
to that day! I long for a life through which Your will and
Your perfect purpose can be accomplished.

Give us this day our daily bread.
And forgive us our debts,
as we forgive our debtors.
And lead us not into temptation,
but deliver us from evil…
—Matthew 6:11–13

FOUR

Our Daily Bread

We've seen so far that prayer is based upon a relationship with God that includes a heart of worship. God is our Father, and in our prayers, we are to express our desire to live for His name and to see His kingdom and His will accomplished in our lives. We shift now from worshipping and praising God in prayer to making requests. To some people, the idea of asking things of God seems a little selfish. If we are living for our Father, however, the reality is that we'll need some resources to do His will and stay on track as we go.

Every once in a while, an urgent need arises in all of our lives. One night while at home watching a championship basketball game from the comfort of my couch, I suddenly experienced a serious need for ice cream. To my dismay, there was none to be found in the house. I asked my daughter Jessica to run to the store and meet this need. She replied, "I'm going to need some money." That was not a selfish request. She was willing to do what I asked; she just needed my help along the way.

There is no doubt that prayer helps us; however, prayer is about bringing glory to God. There is no higher form of personal worship than entering into the presence of God through prayer and readily confessing to Him that we can't make it apart from His blessing on and provision in our lives. When needs arise, it is imperative that we know where to go so that they can be met. Missing out on this truth will greatly limit the help available to us during those times.

I heard a story once about a woman who was in labor with her first child. Her husband called 911, and the operator began arranging for an ambulance to escort the couple to the nearest hospital.

"Where do you live?" asked the operator.

"Eucalyptus Drive," he replied hastily.

"Can you spell it and give me a house number?"

The husband was so nervous and distracted that his mind went blank. After a pause, he countered, "How about

I just take my wife over to Oak Street, and you pick us up there?"

This man had a need, and he knew who to call on to get that need met, but he wasn't quite sure how to articulate it. This problem didn't just affect him—his wife was impacted as well. It is important to remember this because each of us has multiple roles in others' lives. We are fathers/mothers, daughters/sons, husbands/wives, siblings, and friends. God has designed us to go to Him to get our needs met so that we can live for Him in all of the roles He's given us.

Prayer is the avenue through which we must travel to get what we need from God. Asking for those things is not selfish when we remember that our prayers begin by praising God and asking that His agenda and will be accomplished in our lives. We learn in the book of James that God is not in the habit of answering selfish prayers.

> Ye ask, and receive not, because ye ask amiss, that ye may consume it upon your lusts.—James 4:3

If our requests are based on a selfish desire, we are asking "amiss," and the Bible says we'll "receive not." But He delights in giving those things for which we go to Him with humble hearts seeking to carry out His will in our lives.

Provision for Our Needs

Give us this day our daily bread.—Matthew 6:11

As the verse above indicates, we are to go to God in prayer for "our daily bread," but this request is about much more than food. It's about asking for the provision—the tangible and present needs—that arise daily in our lives.

Asking for provision does not mean that we must daily convince or coerce God to act on our behalf to meet those needs. This prayer is recognition that as our Father, God longs to meet our needs and we are going to Him as His children who can't make it without Him. Nothing honors our Father like going to Him in faith believing that He is good and generous and eager to supply our needs.

Let us therefore come boldly unto the throne of grace, that we may obtain mercy, and find grace to help in time of need.—Hebrews 4:16

Be encouraged today with this thought: the God who created the world and all that exists in it can handle any need that arises in your life. Do you need food? He can handle it. Do you have a financial or emotional need? He can do that, too. Our God can do anything but fail, and He has established time and time again that He is a generous and giving Father.

Notice the word *daily* in this text. Our God wants us to meet with Him each day in prayer to get what we need to sustain us for that moment. Too often we want to try to live on yesterday's bread or worry about tomorrow's bread. But yesterday's bread gets stale and moldy, and none of us can know what we'll need tomorrow. Let yesterday and tomorrow go. The bread that God gives is to meet our needs today. As King David said,

> God is our refuge and strength, A very present help in trouble.—Psalm 46:1

Of course, God lives outside the realm of time; He is present in our yesterdays and He is already in tomorrow, but He wants us to enjoy the gift of now. That is why we call it "the present"—it is truly a gift.

> Call unto me, and I will answer thee, and shew thee great and mighty things, which thou knowest not.
> —Jeremiah 33:3

> And whatsoever ye shall ask in my name, that will I do, that the Father may be glorified in the Son. If ye shall ask any thing in my name, I will do it.—John 14:13–14

> And all things, whatsoever ye shall ask in prayer, believing, ye shall receive.—Matthew 21:22

How wonderful to be told repeatedly through the Bible that our requests to our Father can be made with the understanding that He'll meet them, not only because He's a good God, but because He promised.

Forgiving and Being Forgiven

> And forgive us our debts, as we forgive our debtors.
> —Matthew 6:12

I've never met anyone who actually liked debt, and with good reason. Debt holds us back. It costs us interest. And sometimes we find that the thing we went into debt for cost us much more than we ever would have been willing to pay had we only read the fine print. We all have spiritual debt in the form of sin. Judicially, at the moment of salvation that debt is erased; we are completely forgiven of every sin in our past, present, and future. God declares us righteous and our standing before Him perfect and perfectly secure:

> Being justified freely by his grace through the redemption that is in Christ Jesus: Whom God hath set

forth to be a propitiation through faith in his blood, to
declare his righteousness for the remission of sins that
are past, through the forbearance of God; To declare,
I say, at this time his righteousness: that he might be
just, and the justifier of him which believeth in Jesus.
Where is boasting then? It is excluded. By what law?
of works? Nay: but by the law of faith. Therefore we
conclude that a man is justified by faith without the
deeds of the law.—Romans 3:24–28

Although believers are saved from the penalty of
sin, we still battle with bodies that like sin. So while our
relationship with God is safe through faith, our sin or
"debt" load affects our fellowship, holds us back, and costs
us interest in spiritual things. We find encouragement in
Matthew 6:12 to deal with our debt the right way—the way
God does. He doesn't want us to try to hide it because that
never works.

But if ye will not do so, behold, ye have sinned against
the Lord: and be sure your sin will find you out.
—Numbers 32:23

God wants us to recognize and judge our own sin and
bring it into the open by talking to Him.

For if we would judge ourselves, we should not be
judged.—1 Corinthians 11:31

The Way to Pray

God loves us so much that He steps in as a good Father would and corrects us when we skip this process:

> For whom the LORD loveth he correcteth; Even as a father the son in whom he delighteth.—Proverbs 3:12

Parenting looks much different now that my daughters are grown, but there was a time years ago in the Chappell house when a "debt" was owed. We held an impromptu family meeting and I brought up the debt. I was prepared to do one of two things depending on my daughters' responses. First, I was ready to go into correction mode, lovingly dropping a nuclear bomb on a couple of little heads to emphasize that the debt was bad. My alternate plan, should the girls have acknowledged they were in the wrong and agreed with my assessment of the situation, was to just let the whole thing go. Thankfully for all, there were no bombs dropped that night; rather, with lesson learned and ways mended, we enjoyed the rest of our evening.

Life works in a similar way in our relationship with God. But did you notice that the prayer reads "...forgive us our debts *as we forgive our debtors*"? Just as parents notice when their kids are squabbling, God notices when we harbor a grudge against others—and it affects our fellowship with Him.

> For if ye forgive men their trespasses, your heavenly
> Father will also forgive you: But if ye forgive not men
> their trespasses, neither will your Father forgive your
> trespasses.—Matthew 6:14–15

We live in a world of real people with real and serious hurts. Some have wounds that are years old while others' wounds are as fresh as perhaps this week. And without minimizing the circumstances that occasioned these wounds, it is important to realize that we will never be able to get beyond an offense until we forgive those who caused it.

> Moreover if thy brother shall trespass against thee, go
> and tell him his fault between thee and him alone:
> if he shall hear thee, thou hast gained thy brother.
> —Matthew 18:15

If the offender refuses to acknowledge what was done, we can leave it with the Lord, which frees us to begin the process of moving past it whether or not we get that acknowledgment.

Perhaps you are thinking, "Well, that's all fine and good for other people. But you just don't know what they did to me. You don't know what I've been through." And you're right; I don't know your particular situation. But I do know that our relationship with Christ will never be all that it should be if we are not right with the people in our lives. We have not just been called to pray the Lord's Prayer; we've been called to be like Jesus.

> And be ye kind one to another, tenderhearted, *forgiving one another*, even as God for Christ's sake hath forgiven you.—Ephesians 4:32

We are never more like Christ than when we offer forgiveness to someone who does not deserve it.

Getting Protection in Temptation

> And lead us not into temptation, but deliver us from evil…—Matthew 6:13

There's a story told of a man who had been bullied regularly as a child. "There used to be this bully who would demand my lunch money every day. Since I was smaller, I would give it to him. Then I decided to fight back. I started taking karate lessons. But then the karate lesson guy said I had to start paying him five dollars a lesson. So I just went back to paying the bully."[1]

Unfortunately, many Christians choose this man's route when faced with the reality of Satan's tricks and the temptations that come their way. It often seems easier to just pay the bully than to learn how to fight him. But in the text above Jesus asserts that a healthy prayer life is an integral part of seeing victory over temptation.

While God may test us, He does not lead us down paths that end in sin:

> Let no man say when he is tempted, I am tempted of God: for God cannot be tempted with evil, neither tempteth he any man:—James 1:13

But as we travel these paths we find a lot of off ramps that do lead us to sin. When we pray "Lead us not into temptation, but deliver us from evil," we are asking God for strength and wisdom to know which way to go and what to do.

Temptation can seem in some ways like the ocean's tide. During different seasons or with a shift in weather, the pull of the tide changes. The pull is stronger at some times than others, but it would be a mistake to try and measure the strength of the tide by letting it pull you with it. Its strength is better measured as you hold your ground. Similarly, those who know the most about temptation are not those who give in to it, but those who stand against it.

Every year it seems, those of us living in California deal with the threat of wildfires that cost thousands of people their homes. In recent years, these fires have gotten bigger and worse than ever; the fires in 2017-2020 alone account for over 60 percent of the structural losses recorded in the last fifteen years.[2] I'm so thankful for the many thousands of brave firefighters locally and around the country who answer the call to help in California's times of need. They willingly place their lives at risk to rescue the public from the numerous issues that wildfires bring. Their sacrifice, time after time, is for the benefit of others.

Jesus did the same and more for us. His death was the price paid to settle our sin debt, but He rose from the dead and assures us that if we pray in faith, He'll give us the help we need when temptation and evil come to our lives. As with all our requests, we can't succeed without Christ because temptation is a spiritual battlefield:

> For we wrestle not against flesh and blood, but against principalities, against powers, against the rulers of the darkness of this world, against spiritual wickedness in high places.—Ephesians 6:12

Even greater than our need is the power that we find in Christ.

Praying always with all prayer and supplication in the
Spirit, and watching thereunto with all perseverance
and supplication for all saints;—Ephesians 6:18

Prayer is that all-encompassing act of faith that ushers
us into God's presence and brings Him into the arena of our
need. When we pray for God to pardon our debts, we are
dealing with our past. When we pray for provision for our
daily bread, we are dealing with the present. Finally, when
we pray for God to protect us from temptation and evil, we
are looking ahead to the future.

We all have basic human needs, but our greatest need
is a relationship with a Father who can meet all our needs
and then some. He loves us and invites us to enter into His
presence and experience for ourselves the joy of knowing
Him and walking with Him throughout our lives.

Father, the way You meet my needs on a daily basis is
humbling. Thank You for Your loving kindness. I pray that my
forgiveness to others would be reflective of the forgiveness
that You've shown to me. May I stand by Your power
when the temptations come.

…For thine is the kingdom, and the power,
and the glory, for ever. Amen.
—Matthew 6:13

FIVE

Amen

I'll never forget the day, many years ago now, that I sat down with the pastor for whom I worked and shared with Him that I believed God was leading me from my position on his staff to start a church on the West Coast. He asked several questions and generally sought to better understand my heart. As our conversations gave way to making plans, he told me to remember one thing: "Although it matters what you did while you were here, people will remember you most for how you leave." He went on to encourage me to finish my time there well.

While I did not yet have his years of perspective and experience, I understood what he meant. A poor finish would have undermined everything I'd stood and worked for up to that point. I took his advice to heart and pushed through the finish line faithfully so that on my last day I knew I had truly done my best.

In a similar sense, the way we finish our prayers is of great importance. In fact, the final word should really be our first concern. As we see in the text above, Jesus used the word *Amen* to conclude His model prayer. This is not a strange word for many of us, and it's used 150 times throughout the Bible. Those familiar with Scripture will also recognize it as one of the last words uttered by Jesus as He hung on the cross and as the final word in the Bible.

We sometimes think *Amen* is a synonym of *goodbye,* such as we would use to end a phone conversation. We tend to think of it as our way of telling God, "Over and out." In reality, however, *Amen* is much more important. It means, "So be it," "let it be," "I affirm it," and "for a truth."[1] We see this meaning in Paul's writing:

> For all the promises of God in him are yea, and in him Amen, unto the glory of God by us.
> —2 Corinthians 1:20

When we close our prayers with "Amen," we are saying, "God, we believe Your words are truth and we want to see Your will done in our time and in our lives. We've brought our needs to You, and now we are trusting You with them because we know that You will do what is best." This word conveys a powerful meaning about the One to whom we offer our prayer in faith.

He Is Preeminent

...For thine is the kingdom... —2 Corinthians 1:20

The entertainment industry loves to make superlative lists that assign rankings according to some perceived level of importance. A quick Google search will give you lists of the "fifty most beautiful people," the "top ten wealthiest families in the world," or the "top Instagram influencers to follow."

One ranking that may be unfamiliar to many is "most watched animal on YouTube." The current record holder for that illustrious title is Motimaru the cat, a gray Scottish Fold from Japan whose recorded antics racked up nearly 700 million views between December 2019 and September 2021. For his efforts, Motimaru earned a Guinness World Record and was signed to a talent management firm.[1]

No person, event, or animal in these silly rankings will ever come close to matching the importance of Jesus, God the Son. The final clause in the Lord's Prayer acknowledges that God is completely and entirely in charge. He is not just prominent; He is preeminent.

> And he is the head of the body, the church: who is the beginning, the firstborn from the dead; that in all things he might have the preeminence.
> —Colossians 1:18

This is so encouraging because as we look around the world, we see total chaos: wars and rumors of war, political upheaval, the devastation of natural disasters, and countless millions around the world who are starving at this moment because of famine and pestilence. Right here in America the last few years have brought devaluation of our assets, increasing cost of commodities, and a complete lack of cohesion in our government on both foreign and domestic issues. The principles that led our nation to greatness are being abandoned at a breakneck pace, and one can't help but wonder if this is rooted in ignorance or something more insidious.

But we can be encouraged by this: at the end of the day, and in spite of the chaos that man perpetuates, God is still on the throne and truly in control. The mess of the world is not a testimony to the inattention of God, but rather to His prophetic Word. God will right all wrongs and bring justice where it is wanting. As the psalmist wrote,

Thy throne, O God, is for ever and ever: The sceptre of
thy kingdom is a right scepter.—Psalm 45:6

Remember, when Jesus taught the principles of prayer
in our text passage, He was speaking to a group of Jewish
disciples who were living in a world controlled by a Roman
emperor. As they were essentially subservient to a system
of heavy-handed governance, these men would have
wondered and been filled with joyful hope at the truth that
God, not Caesar, was in control. To them it appeared that
Rome ruled the day, yet God used it all for the furtherance
of His message of salvation.

Things in this world will not long wallow in chaos. An
end is coming, and everything will happen just as God said
it would. He will come again, as He promised.

And the seventh angel sounded; and there were
great voices in heaven, saying, The kingdoms of this
world are become the kingdoms of our Lord, and
of his Christ; and he shall reign for ever and ever.
—Revelation 11:15

I can praise God in prayer because as His child I am a
citizen of Heaven.

> For our conversation is in heaven; from whence
> also we look for the Saviour, the Lord Jesus Christ:
> —Philippians 3:20

This earth is an outpost; my Father is coming again to reign forever and ever.

He Is Powerful

> …and the power… —2 Corinthians 1:20

The Greek word used in Matthew 6:13 to mean *power* is *dunamis,* from which we get our word *dynamite.*[2] God's power is more than enough to completely dismantle any trouble that we face.

> Ah Lord GOD! behold, thou hast made the heaven
> and the earth by thy great power and stretched
> out arm, and there is nothing too hard for thee.
> —Jeremiah 32:17

I like the story of the little boy travelling alone on a plane who was amusing himself by drawing on some papers he pulled from his backpack. The man sitting next to him noticed the papers were from a Sunday School lesson and, surmising that the boy attended church the man said, "Son, if you can tell me something that God can do I'll give you an apple." As the man held a shiny apple before him, the boy considered it thoughtfully. Then he told the man, "If you can tell me something God *can't* do, I'll give you a whole barrel of apples." The boy had it right! God's power is not simply enough to meet our needs; it's more than enough. We can rejoice because He is the one who can "do exceeding abundantly above" anything we could imagine (Ephesians 3:20).

Years ago I worked for an aerospace company called Apeiron Technology, Inc. My position involved, among other things, some sales work. I would call an airline or prospective customer to persuade them that Apeiron provided services that could help them in their daily operations. More than a few times I would call a company and go through the process of sharing our service only to hear, "Sounds good, but it's out of my hands." I quickly learned how imperative it was that I was connected to the right person when I made these calls. I didn't want to waste my time giving a sales pitch to someone without the power to make a decision on behalf of the company.

When we go to God in prayer, we can rest assured that there is no manager or supervisor we should be speaking to instead. We are talking to the only One in the universe with the power needed to do anything that needs to be done in us and through us.

He Is Working for Our Good

...and the glory, for ever. Amen. —2 Corinthians 1:20

It is important to realize that when we praise God in prayer we are not just praising Him for what He does, but for who He is. He is a glorious God.

O LORD our Lord, How excellent is thy name in all the earth! Who hast set thy glory above the heavens. —Psalm 8:1

The glory of God is more a state of being than an action. It is more of an attribute of His person than a characteristic of His power. This speaks of His nature. If God were preeminent and powerful, but not good, benevolent, or glorious, our requests would never touch His heart. But our God is a God of love. When we talk to Him, we are talking to the One who longs to make the right decision for our good. And not only does He have the ability to help us, but He invites us to go to Him. It is His nature to hear our prayers and to do that which is best for us.

Do you have someone in your life with whom you have an open invitation to come any time that you're in need of support, advice, or help? For me, one of those people is my older brother, Paul. Some years back I needed some advice and really wanted to talk the matter over with my brother. I told my wife I was going to go visit Paul and when she asked why I said simply, "Because he'll help me." He had no idea what I was going through, but he'd once told me, "If I can ever do anything for you, just let me know." And I knew he meant it. There's a sense of trust and comfort when I remember that any time that I have a need, my brother will do his best to help.

With God, we find a relationship with One that we can go to at any time and know He can do something about everything we could possibly be going through. No problem on Earth is too great for Him. And then we add the final words from our text: "for ever. Amen." This highlights the glorious person of God, who never changes:

For I am the LORD, I change not.—Malachi 3:6

In an ever-changing world, we have a constant in God. We can go to Him in prayer and know beyond a shadow of a doubt that we have His attention. And what's more, we find our attentive, unchanging God is powerful—able to change things through our sincere prayer.

In more than twenty years as pastor of Coastline Baptist Church, I've been privileged to pray with and for the church over countless things. Together we've petitioned God about new buildings, new jobs, new relationships, marital troubles, health problems, financial difficulties, parenting challenges—you name it. Countless times I've been overjoyed to see and hear the ways God has answered our prayers and worked miracles before our eyes. But there have also been times that we didn't see God work in the way we were praying He would.

There's a lesson to learn in the way we respond to God's answers to our prayers. I still remember speaking to one man who had attended the church, but had not been seen in a few weeks. I called him to make sure all was well, and he told me, "I'm not coming back. I don't believe in this stuff anymore." When I asked why, he replied, "Because I prayed, and God didn't answer my prayer."

As many of us do, this man had missed the point of the final word of Christ's prayer. He missed the understanding that God is in charge and will—from His heart of love—do the right thing for our lives every time, even if we can't see it in the moment.

You see, prayer is not our going to God to tell Him what to do. Prayer aligns our will to God's as we humbly talk with Him, knowing that He will take our prayers and filter them through His will. It is offering our praise to God, delivering our petitions to God, and accepting by faith His decision. When we say "Amen," we are saying, "I trust You."

The Pursuit of a Lifetime

The Lord's Prayer is built upon a relationship with God by faith. It honors the sovereignty of God, longs for His purposes to be accomplished in our lives and the world, seeks our daily provisions, affords us the joy of God's forgiveness, and secures safety from temptation. It begins and ends with praise for a God who loves us and offers us a way to draw closer to Him daily to see our needs met and our lives strengthened to give Him glory.

I hope you have been helped and challenged through this close look at the Lord's Prayer and that what we have studied together will encourage you to *pray*. If prayer was critical enough for Jesus to spend time teaching us about, we can rest assured that prayer deserves our pursuit for a lifetime.

The Way to Pray

Father, may I live by the power of Your Spirit and not by the feeble, ineffective power of my flesh. I pray that my actions would daily bring You glory. Thank You that You have a plan—and a place for me in Your plan.

Make me a clean vessel through which Your will can be accomplished and draw me closer to You as I obey Your command and example in establishing a life of prayer.

In Jesus' name,
Amen

Endnotes

Chapter 1

1   "American Time Use Survey—May to December 2019 and 2020 Results," *Bureau of Labor Statistics,* July 22, 2021, https://www.bls.gov/news.release/pdf/atus.pdf.

2   "Personal Development Market Size, Share & Trends Analysis Report By Instrument (Books, e-Platforms, Personal Coaching/Training, Workshops), By Focus Area, By Region, And Segment Forecasts, 2020–2027," *Grand View Research,* July 2020, https://www.grandviewresearch.com/industry-analysis/personal-development-market.

Chapter 2

1   Luca Pancani, Marco Marinucci, Nicolas Aureli, and Paolo Riva, "Forced Social Isolation and Mental Health: A Study on 1,006 Italians Under COVID-19 Lockdown," *Frontiers in Psychology,* Volume 12, 2021, https://www.frontiersin.org/article/10.3389/fpsyg.2021.663799.

2   G. M. Cocoris, *Evangelism: A Biblical Approach* (Chicago, IL: Moody Publishers, 1984), 108.

Chapter 3

1   James Strong, *The New Strong's Exhaustive Concordance of the Bible,* (Nashville, TN: Thomas Nelson, Inc., 1991), entry 37.

Chapter 4

1   Jack Handey, *Fuzzy Memories,* Kansas City, MO: Andrews McMeel Publishing, 1996), np.

2   "Wildfires Destroy Thousands of Structures Each Year," *Headwaters Economics,* November 2020, https://headwaterseconomics.org/natural-hazards/structures-destroyed-by-wildfire/.

Chapter 5

1   James Strong, *The New Strong's Exhaustive Concordance of the Bible,* (Nashville, TN: Thomas Nelson, Inc., 1991), entry 281.

2   "Japanese Scottish Fold Motimaru Grabs Guinness Gold Record for Most Watched Cat on YouTube," *Sora News 24,* September 8, 2021, https://soranews24.com/2021/09/08/japanese-scottish-fold-motimaru-grabs-guinness-world-record-for-most-watched-cat-on-youtube/.

ABOUT THE AUTHOR

STEPHEN CHAPPELL is the senior pastor of Coastline Baptist Church in Oceanside, California. Having a burden to see people saved and churches planted on the West Coast, he and his family moved to northern San Diego County in July of 1998 to begin this work. The Lord is using Coastline Baptist to make an impact on their community. Stephen is the author of numerous books including *The Heart of the Shepherd* and *Lessons from the Road* and is also a frequent speaker offering encouragement and biblical insight for life. Serving with his wife Lisa, Stephen seeks to encourage people of faith to boldly live for God.

ADDITIONAL BOOKS BY STEPHEN CHAPPELL

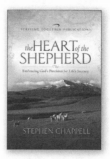

The Heart of the Shepherd
Embracing God's Provision for Life's Journey

By Stephen Chappell

In these pages, Pastor Stephen Chappell explores the twenty-third Psalm with insight that will delight, strengthen, energize, and comfort every Christian.

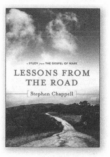

Lessons from the Road
A Study from the Gospel of Mark

By Stephen Chappell

Including historical background, cross references, and clear applications, this verse-by-verse study of the Gospel of Mark will focus your attention on your Savior and captivate your heart with His incredible power and love.

Offensive Faith
Taking Your Faith on the Offense in a World Trying to Keep you on the Defense

By Jeremy Stalnecker and Stephen Chappell

Each chapter in this captivating book will encourage and challenge you to boldly live out your faith and purposefully share the gospel.

ADDITIONAL RESOURCES FOR SPIRITUAL GROWTH

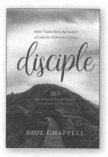

Disciple
Daily Truths from the Gospel of Luke
for Followers of Jesus

By Paul Chappell

These brief devotions will draw you closer to
the Lord and encourage you to follow Jesus in
practical ways throughout each day.

Journey through the New Testament
90-Day Devotional

By Tim Christoson

From Matthew to Revelation, each daily
reading will help you develop a deeper
relationship with the Lord and a greater
understanding of His Word.

Victory
A Seven-Step Strategy for Resisting
Temptation and Overcoming Sin

By Jim Schettler

Discover seven practical steps you can take
to overcome sin and live the victorious
Christian life.